A DAY IN THE LIFE OF A
Police Detective

by David Paige

photography by Roger Ruhlin

Troll Associates

Library of Congress Catalog Card Number: 80-54102
ISBN 0-89375-442-0   ISBN 0-89375-443-9 Paper Edition

The author and publisher wish to thank the Chicago Police Department, Acting Superintendent Joseph DiLeonardi;
Director of News Affairs, Tina Vicini; and Homicide investigator Paul Roppel; Jerome T. Burke, Judge, Circuit Court
of Cook County; Captain Jay Oliver, Chicago Fire Department; Perry Smulson and Spencer Ruhlin, for their
generous assistance and cooperation.

At eight in the morning, Detective Paul Roppel
signs in for work at the station house. Paul is a
homicide detective. He investigates crimes in
which someone has been killed. He wears "plain"
clothes, and does some of his work at his desk.

Paul and his partner are working on a case in which a truck was hijacked and later abandoned. The truck driver was murdered, and a gun was found near his body. Fingerprints have already been taken from the gun. Now it will go to a police laboratory for further tests.

When the abandoned truck was located, some old clothes were found in the bushes nearby. Although they may or may not have anything to do with the crime, Paul enters in his report the hat and shoe sizes. Then these articles will be sent to the police lab.

Tests on the gun are already under way. Paul checks in at the police lab to watch the ballistics tests. The ballistics expert fires the weapon into a box filled with cotton wadding.

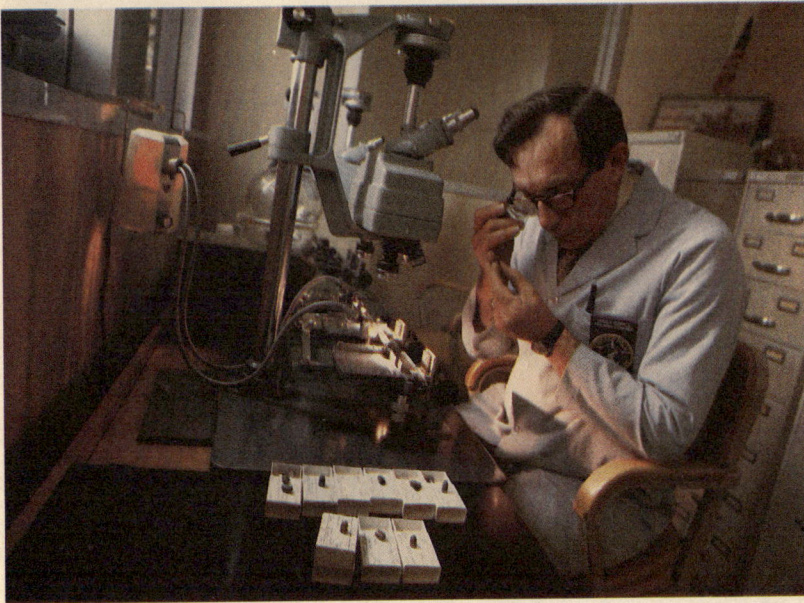

The bullet is removed from the wadding, then examined under a microscope. Does it have the same marks as those on the bullet used to kill the victim? It does, so this gun is probably the murder weapon. And the murderer is probably the person whose fingerprints were found on the gun.

Fingerprints from the murder weapon are matched against those in the department files. The fingerprint section also works with the FBI, which has the fingerprints of millions of people. The FBI files will be used in this case, because the prints from the gun do not match any prints in the department files.

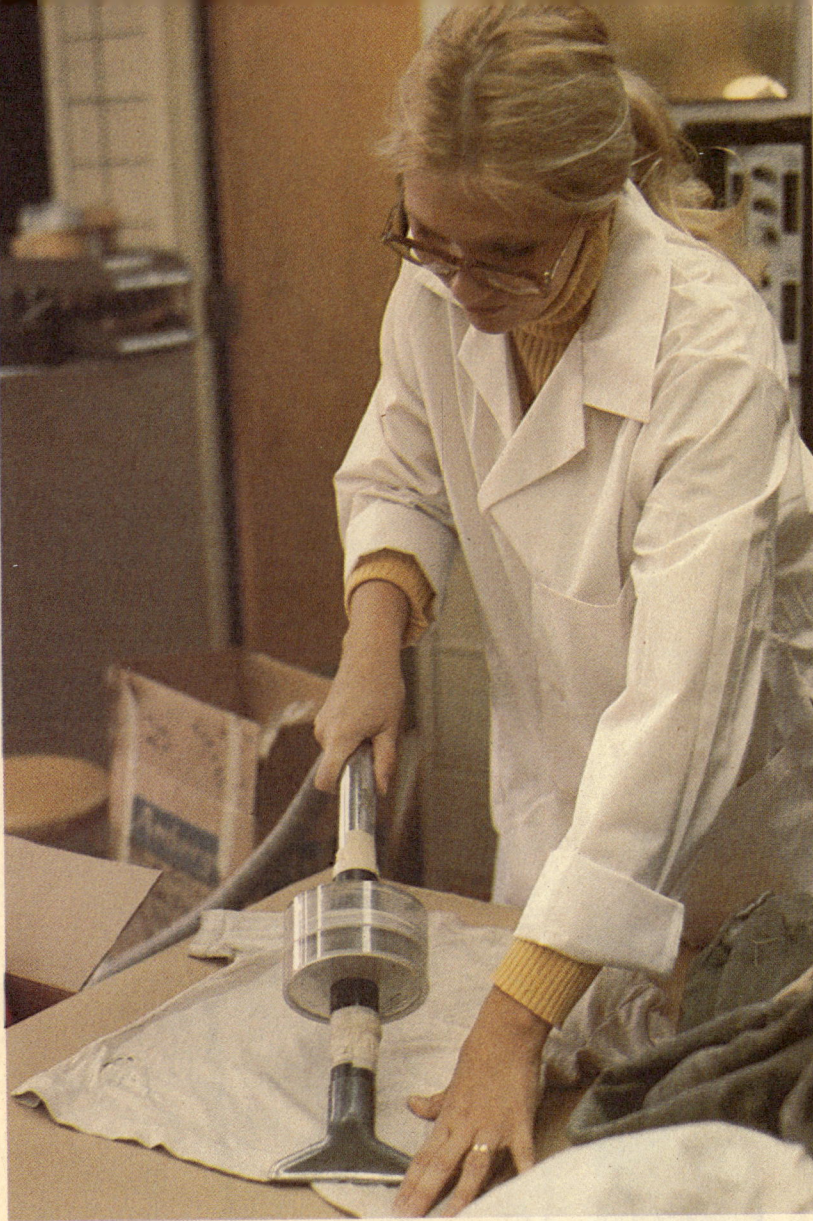

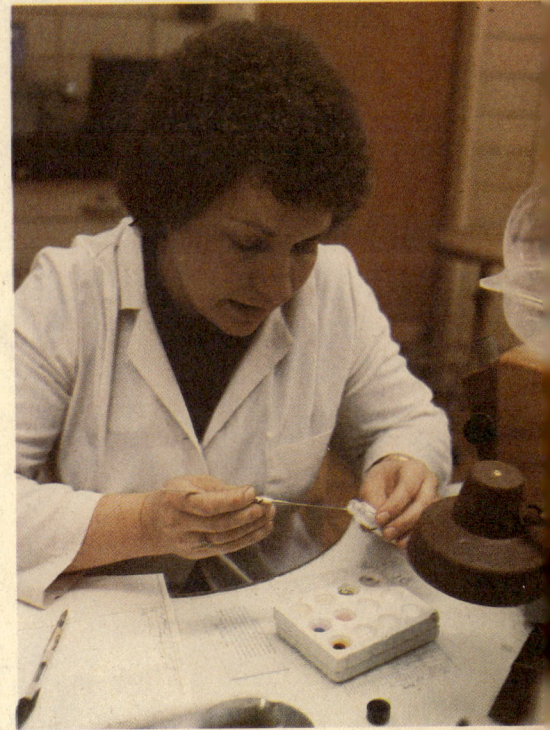

In another laboratory, technicians vacuum the victim's clothing. The dust they collect might contain bits of hair, skin, or other clues to the hijacker's identity. Bloodstains are checked and matched to the victim's blood type in the chemical analysis laboratory.

Before Paul can do any more work on this case, the commanding officer calls him into his office. A body has been found in the debris of a fire. It may turn out to be an accident, but the police must investigate to determine the cause of the fire and the cause of death.

Paul and his partner use an unmarked car. It is equipped with police communication equipment so the detectives can tell headquarters where they are, and where they are going. Paul checks in with headquarters as they arrive at the burned-out building.

A uniformed police officer guards the building. He says that the custodian was apparently overcome by smoke. The body has been taken to the morgue, where the cause of death will be established and the identity of the man will be checked.

Paul learns that a scorched gasoline can has been found at the back of the building—where the fire started. This fire may be a case of arson—that is, someone may have started the fire on purpose. If so, the custodian's death was not just an accident. The charge could be manslaughter, or even murder.

Headquarters sends an "evidence technician" from the Mobile Crime Unit. Wearing rubber gloves, the technician helps the detectives sift through the debris. Evidence technicians are experts, trained to gather facts that others might never notice at the scene of a crime.

Once the gasoline can is safely wrapped and locked away, the evidence technician gathers burnt material for laboratory analysis. The laboratory will determine the temperature at which the material burned. Fires started with gasoline burn at unusually high temperatures.

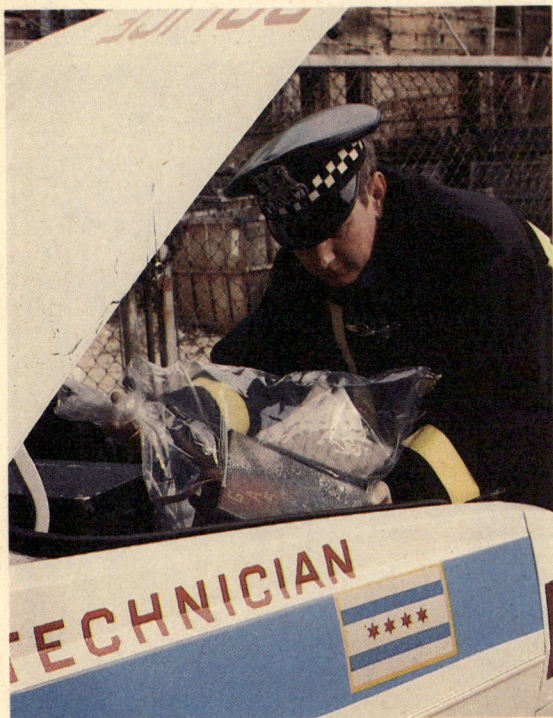

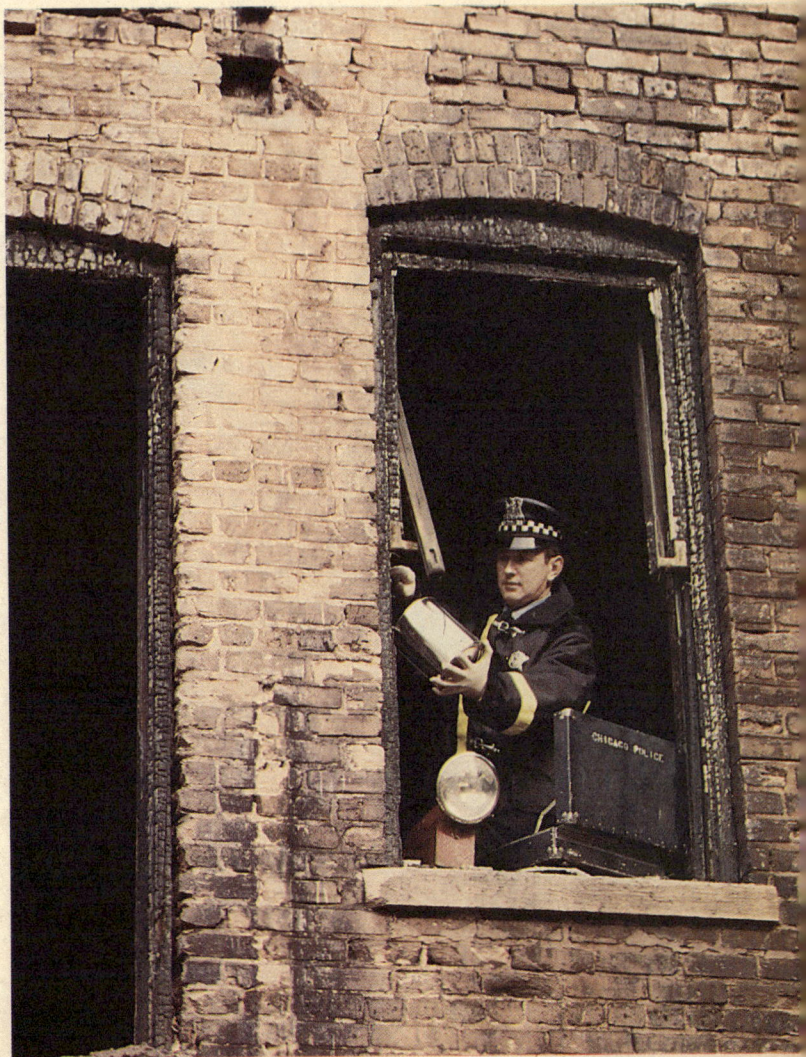

Paul begins the long job of interviewing witnesses. One woman points to where she first saw smoke coming from a window. Only minutes before that, she says, she saw some young men outside the building. Even more important, she thinks she recognized one of them. Paul listens carefully to her description.

Paul stops to talk to the fire chief. The chief has been to hundreds of fires. He is an expert on how fires start—or are started. Later, Paul will also have to interview the owner and tenants of the burned building.

All the evidence Paul gathers from interviews and laboratory tests is used when criminal suspects are tried. Today Paul must appear in court to give the facts in a case he investigated many months ago. Like all other witnesses, he must be sworn in.

Paul is a witness for the prosecution. He tells the details of his investigation—what evidence he found, what the laboratory tests have shown, and what he has learned about the suspect. Then he is cross-examined by the suspect's lawyer. The jury, not the police, must decide a suspect's innocence or guilt.

After his testimony is given, Paul is free to leave the court. When he was a boy, he knew he wanted a career in law enforcement. He had dreamed of training police dogs, or flying a police helicopter. But by the time he entered the police academy, he knew that what he really wanted was to become a homicide detective.

In his office back at headquarters, Paul receives a telephone call from his partner. He discovers that his partner has turned up some new developments in the arson case. They now know the identity and the address of the man who was seen just before the fire began.

Paul picks up his partner, and they go to the young man's address. He is not there, but a neighbor says the suspect often hangs around with his friends on a certain street corner a few blocks away.

Information provided by ordinary citizens is often helpful to the police. There on the corner, just as the neighbor said, is a young man who matches the description Paul got that morning. Before doing anything else, Paul calls headquarters. He requests a police wagon for help in making the arrest.

The call comes in to a computer panel board at central headquarters. Each panel board is a map of a portion of the city. Police cars are represented as white dots. The red dots are the cars of police supervisors. The operators can see the location of every police car at any moment of the day or night.

When someone calls the police to ask for help or to report a crime, the call is directed to the person whose map board covers that area. When Paul's call comes in, an operator sees where Paul's car is located, and she dispatches a police wagon to the scene.

Once Paul knows that help is on the way, he approaches the young man and identifies himself. Paul looks relaxed and speaks politely, but should there be trouble, his hand is only a split-second away from the gun in his shoulder holster.

Paul searches the suspect to be sure he is not carrying a weapon. Then Paul tells him he is under arrest, and reads him his rights. Suspects have the right to have a lawyer with them when they are questioned, or even to refuse to answer questions at all.

As two officers from the police wagon approach, Paul handcuffs the suspect. Paul explains to the young man that he is suspected of being involved in a fire that morning. He will not be formally charged with a crime until the police have questioned him.

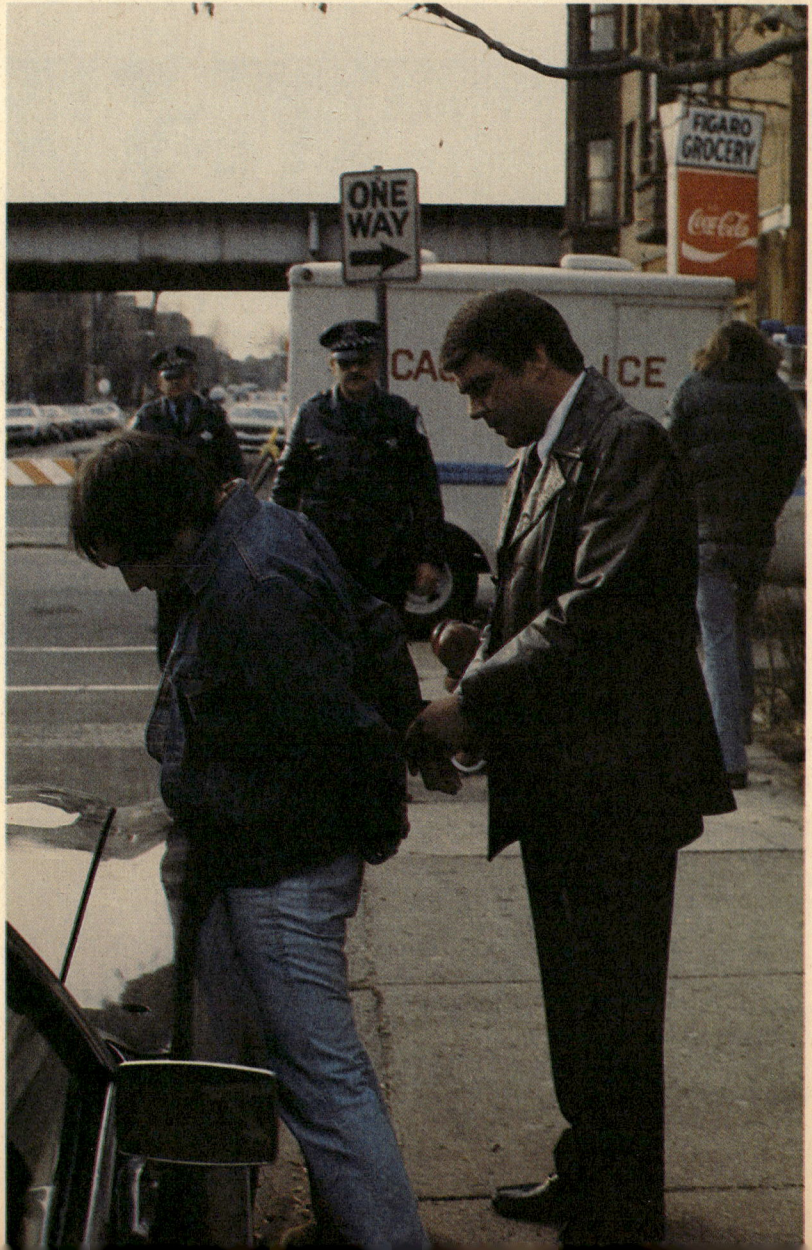

The suspect is led into the wagon and the doors are locked behind him. Paul and his partner drive back to the station, followed by the police wagon. In an emergency, the detectives would have handled the arrest alone, but they are always relieved when there is time to summon extra help.

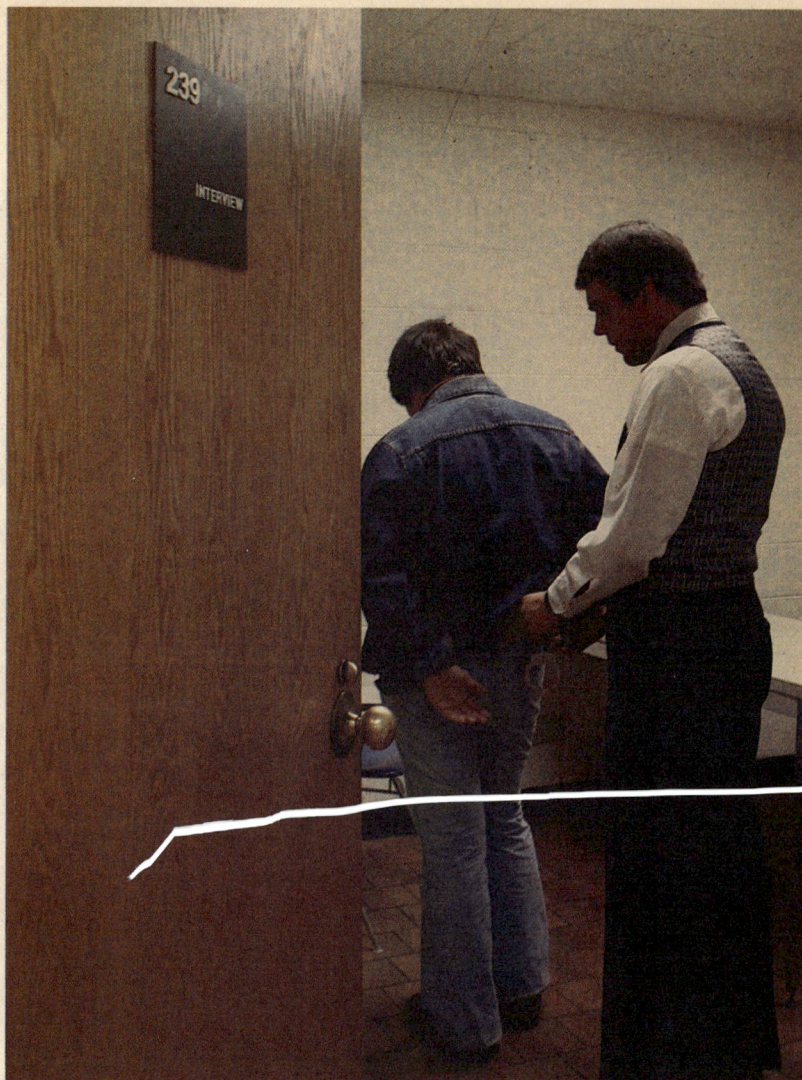

At the station, the man is told that charges of arson and manslaughter could be brought against him. He is fingerprinted, and taken to an interview room. Here Paul and other officers will question him to find out his side of the story. This is an important part of trying to get all the facts in a case.

By the end of Paul's shift, the suspicious fire and the death it caused have not yet been solved. The man Paul arrested is still only a suspect, who will remain innocent until proven guilty in a court of law. The lab tests have not yet led to any suspects in the hijacking-murder case. Police work is done slowly and carefully.

But the work of a police officer never stops. Off duty—home with his family, or even on vacation—Paul must wear his gun and carry his identification at all times. Helping people and protecting them is Paul's business—all day, every day.